The author, illustrator and
publisher would like to thank
Heather Angel, MSc, for her
advice and guidance in
the preparation of this book.

First published 2007 by Walker Books Ltd
87 Vauxhall Walk, London SE11 5HJ

This edition published 2009

2 4 6 8 10 9 7 5 3 1

Text © 2007 Nick Dowson
Illustrations © 2007 Yu Rong

The right of Nick Dowson and Yu Rong to be
identified as author and illustrator
respectively of this work has been asserted by
them in accordance with the Copyright,
Designs and Patents Act 1988

This book has been typeset in Green

Printed in China

British Library Cataloguing in
Publication Data:
a catalogue record for this book is available
from the British Library

ISBN 978-1-4063-1871-5

www.walkerbooks.co.uk

For my mum
N. D.

In memory
of my beloved
father
Y. R.

CLASS JF	LOCATION HQ 6/09
AUTHOR DAWSON, Nick	
TITLE Tracks of a Panda	

THIS BOOK IS TO BE RETURNED ON OR BEFORE THE LAST DATE STAMPED BELOW

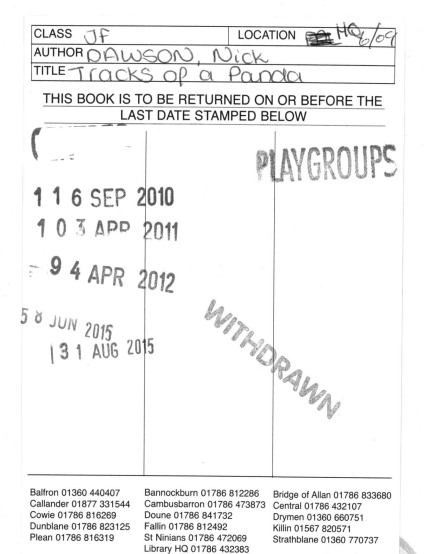

PLAYGROUPS

1 1 6 SEP 2010

1 0 3 APR 2011

9 4 APR 2012

5 8 JUN 2015

1 3 1 AUG 2015

WITHDRAWN

Tracks of a
PANDA

Nick Dowson   illustrated by Yu Rong

WALKER BOOKS
AND SUBSIDIARIES
LONDON · BOSTON · SYDNEY · AUCKLAND

*H*igh on a
mist-wrapped mountain,
cradled in a leafy nest,
Panda holds her newborn cub
gently in her giant paw.

Small as a pine cone,
pink as a blob of
wriggling sunset,
he sinks squawking into
his mother's fur
until her warm milk
fills his mouth.

Panda cubs
are born blind
and almost
furless.
They are
900 times
smaller than
their mothers.

For days Panda stays with her cub
in the hollow tree den.
But the need to feed herself
grows stronger, and
one bright August morning
she leaves him and
follows her old tracks
to the patch of
bamboo grass she eats.

There are
many different
kinds of
bamboo, but
pandas choose
to eat only
a few kinds.

8

Pandas have very big back teeth to help them crush tough bamboo stems.

She rolls on her back in
a soft bed of ferns and grabs a
handful of bamboo.
Slowly her big black nose wrinkles:
these leaves smell good
and she is very hungry.
Before she goes back to cuddle
and suckle her cub,
Panda strips
ten stems bare.

For seven weeks the cub's eyes stay shut.
He feeds and sleeps, cries and gurgles.
While he grows, around his ears and eyes,
across his legs and like a road of
hairy ink on his back,
some of his fur
darkens, like his
mum's, into black.

One autumn day, he crawls up Panda's chest
on to her neck. Something cold and wet
tickles his nose and his eyes open for the
first time – on a world of falling snow.

It takes four years for panda cubs to be as big as their mothers.

The cub grows fast through winter.
He still climbs and plays on his mother, but now he takes
his first steps along the mountain tracks.

But Panda has not eaten well for weeks.
Her bamboo patch is dying. Now that her cub is
six months old and strong enough to travel,
she knows they must find a new home .

Pandas' black and
white fur is good
camouflage in winter.

Below her old territory
the path is steep.
Weak with hunger,
Panda stumbles
and bumps her cub into
a deep drift of snow.

She goes to him and
smells an unexpected
buried meal there.
Snow flies as she scrapes.
This deer meat is old
but full of goodness.

Pandas eat mostly
bamboo, but
sometimes other
things — like insects,
fish or meat.

After eating, Panda
suckles her sleepy cub,
then, thirsty, drinks
from a stream.

A shadow slips through
the trees. Closer it comes,
its long tongue lolling.

Panda lifts her big
dripping head.
Like knives, her long
claws slash the air,
and the wild dog growls
and slinks away.

When they
need to defend
their cubs,
mother pandas
are very fierce.

With danger in the forest,
Panda needs a safe
place to sleep …
in a tree.

She hugs the fir's frosty
trunk with both arms, and
her strong claws and
furry feet grip the bark.
Her cub clings to her
shoulder as they clamber
towards the clouds;
then he leaves
her and scrambles
to his own high perch.

Like other bears,
pandas are very
good climbers.

21

When she wakes, Panda suckles her cub, but still
needs food for herself. They move on.

Soon she sees a new mountain rising,
with bamboo on its slopes.
Cold water laps at her tired feet
and she walks into a
stream's dark pool.

To move from
place to place
in the mountains,
pandas need to
be able to swim.

22

Her paws touch bottom all the way, but in the middle
the cub has to swim. He kicks hard with his feet,
and his paws turn to paddles as he pushes the
water behind him.

Pandas have five "fingers" and a sixth one, more like a thumb, that helps them hold bamboo.

This new territory
has plenty of food.
Panda won't go hungry now.
Her cub, too,
begins to eat bamboo.
He grips a stem and,
copying his mother,
curls his sticky tongue
around the leaves.

Spring brings warm rain, and juicy
new shoots of bamboo poke up.
One day, mother and cub are
feeding when they hear axes thud
and branches crash nearby.
Panda stops chewing.
Villagers are chopping firewood.
If they move up the mountain,
she and her cub cannot stay.

Slowly she climbs up a deer path,
her cub close behind…

Mother pandas
will not share
territory with
other pandas
or people.

Cloud curls around their tracks as they go.
Their hunt for a new home is beginning again.

Index

Look up the pages to find out
about all these panda things.
Don't forget to look at both kinds of
word – **this kind** and this kind.
Look in the pictures too.

About the author

Nick Dowson is a teacher and writer.
He loves wild places and the animals that live
there. "Mountains are where I like to be
the most," he says, "just like the giant panda."

About the illustrator

Yu Rong studied Chinese art in Nanjing
before moving to London to do an
MA at the Royal College of Art. "I've never
seen a wild panda," she says, "but I know
the mountain country where they
like to live."

About pandas

Giant pandas live only in a few high
mountain forests in south-west China.
Because female pandas raise just one cub
at a time, panda numbers are slow to grow.
It does not help that poachers still hunt
them and loggers threaten their habitat.
Where special reserves are set up
to protect them, pandas do well. Even so,
their future survival is at risk: there are
only about 2,500 wild giant pandas left.

大熊猫

Praise for Nature Storybooks...

"For the child who constantly asks How? Why?
and What For? this series is excellent."
The Sunday Express

"A boon to parents seeking non-fiction picture books to read
with their children. They have excellent texts
and a very high standard of illustration to go with them."
The Daily Telegraph

"As books to engage and delight children, they work superbly.
I would certainly want a set in any primary
classroom I was working in."
Times Educational Supplement

"Here are books that stand out from the crowd,
each one real and individual in its own right and
the whole lot as different from most other series non-fiction
as tasty Lancashire is from processed Cheddar."
Books for Keeps

Find notes for teachers about how to use Nature Storybooks in the classroom at
www.walkerbooks.co.uk/naturestorybooks

Nature Storybooks support KS 1-2 Science